LIBRARIES

IN THE

MEDIEVAL AND RENAISSANCE PERIODS.

FIG. 2.   General view of part of the Library attached to the Church of
S. Wallberg at Zutphen.

LIBRARIES

IN THE

MEDIEVAL AND RENAISSANCE PERIODS.

J. W. CLARK, M.A., F.S.A.

REGISTRARY OF THE UNIVERSITY, AND
FORMERLY FELLOW OF TRINITY COLLEGE, CAMBRIDGE.

ARGONAUT, INC., PUBLISHERS
CHICAGO   MCMLXVIII

THE REDE LECTURE,
DELIVERED JUNE 13, 1894

The lecture was illustrated by lantern-slides. A brief notice of each of these is printed in the text in Italics at the place in the lecture where the slide was exhibited.

Manufactured in the United States of America
Unchanged Reprint of the 1894 edition

ARGONAUT INC., PUBLISHERS
737 North Michigan Avenue
Chicago, Illinois 60611

LIBRARIES.

A LIBRARY may be considered from two very different points of view : as a workshop, or as a Museum.

The former commends itself to the practical turn of mind characteristic of the present day; common sense urges that mechanical ingenuity, which has done so much in other directions, should be employed in making the acquisition of knowledge less cumbrous and less tedious; that as we travel by steam, so we should also read by steam, and be helped in our studies by the varied resources of modern invention. There lies on my table at this present moment a *Handbook of Library Appliances,* in which fifty-three closely printed pages are devoted to this interesting subject, with illustrations of various contrivances by which the working of a large library is to be facilitated and brought up to date. In fact, from this point of view a library may be described as a gigantic mincing-machine, into which the labours of the past are flung, to be turned out again in a slightly altered form as the literature of the present.

If, on the other hand, a library be regarded as a Museum—and I use the word in its original sense as a temple or haunt of the Muses —very different ideas are evoked. Such a place is as useful as the other—every facility for study is given—but what I may call the personal element as affecting the treasures there assembled is brought prominently forward. The development of printing, as the result of in- dividual effort; the art of bookbinding, as prac- tised by different persons in different countries; the history of the books themselves, the libraries in which they have found a home, the hands

that have turned their pages, are there taken
note of. Modern literature is fully represented,
but the men of past days are not thrust out
of sight; their footsteps seem to linger in the
rooms where once they walked—their shades
seem to protect the books they once handled.
What Browning felt about frescoes may be
applied—*mutatis mutandis*—to books in such an
asylum as I am trying to portray :

> Wherever a fresco peels and drops,
>   Wherever an outline weakens and wanes
> Till the latest life in the painting stops,
>   Stands One whom each fainter pulse-tick pains :
> One, wishful each scrap should clutch the brick,
>   Each tinge not wholly escape the plaster,
> A lion who dies of an ass's kick,
>   The wronged great soul of an ancient Master.

It may be safely asserted that at no time
has a love of reading, a desire to be fairly well-
informed on all sorts of subjects, been so widely
diffused as at the present day. As a necessary
consequence of this the 'workshop' view of a
library has been very generally accepted. I

have no wish to undervalue it; I only plead
for the recognition of another sentiment which
may at times be overlaid by the pressure
of daily avocations. In Cambridge, at least,
there is no fear that it should ever be obliterated
altogether, for we have effected a happy alliance
between the present and the past, by which
neither is neglected, neither is unduly prominent.
This being the case, it has occurred to me that
I may be so fortunate as to interest a Cambridge
audience while I set before them some of the
results at which I have arrived in investigating
the position, the arrangement, and the fittings
of libraries in the medieval and renaissance
periods.   It will, of course, be impossible to
attempt more than a sketch of so extensive a
subject, and I fear that I must omit the contents
of the bookcases altogether; but I shall hope,
by a selection of typical illustrations, to make
you realise what some of the libraries, monastic,
public, or private, that fall within my period
were like.

I must begin with a few words about Roman libraries, because their methods influenced the Middle Ages, and are, in fact, the precursors of those in fashion in our own times. The Romans preserved their books in two ways : either in a small room or closet, for reading elsewhere ; or in a large apartment, fitted up with greater or less splendour, according to the taste or the means of the possessor, in which the books were doubtless studied as in a modern library. An instructive example of the former class was one of the first discoveries at Herculaneum in 1754. It was a very small room, so small in fact that a man who stood with his arms extended in the centre of it could almost touch the walls on either side, yet 1700 rolls were found in it. These were kept in wooden presses (*armaria*) which stood against the walls like a modern bookcase. Besides these a rectangular case occupied the central space, with only a narrow passage to the right and left between it and the wall-cases. These cases

were about a man's height, and had been
numbered. It may be concluded from this
that a catalogue of the books had once existed.
In larger libraries the books were kept in
similar presses, but they were ornamented with
the busts or pictures of illustrious men, under
each of which was a suitable inscription, usually
in verse.

No ancient figure of one of these book-
presses has been preserved, so far as I have
been able to ascertain ; but, as furniture is apt
to retain its original forms with but little varia-
tion for a very long period, a representation
of a press containing the four Gospels, which
occurs among the mosaics in the Mausoleum of
the Empress Galla Placidia at Ravenna, though
it could not have been executed before the
middle of the fifth century, may be taken as
a fairly accurate picture of the book-presses of
an earlier age. It is unnecessary to describe it,
for it is exactly like a still later example which I
am about to shew you. This picture occurs at

the beginning of the MS. of the Vulgate called the *Codex Amiatinus*, which is now proved to have been written in England, at Wearmouth or Jarrow, but probably by an Italian scribe, shortly before 716. The seated figure represents Ezra writing the Law.

Bookcase in the Codex Amiatinus: from Garrucci, " Storia dell' arte Cristiana," iii. pl. 126.

To get an idea of one of the larger Roman libraries in ancient times we cannot do better than turn to that of the Vatican at the present day. It was fitted up as we see it now—with presses, busts, and antique vases, by Pope Sixtus V., in 1588. It is therefore, at best, only a modern antique ; but arranged so skilfully that an ancient Roman, if he could come to life again, might imagine himself in his own library.

Interior of part of the Vatican Library.

The library-era, as we may call it, of the Christian world, began with the publication of the Rule of S. Benedict, early in the sixth century. But, just as that Rule emphasized and arranged on the lines of an ordered system observances which had long been practised by isolated congregations or individuals living in solitude— so the part of it which deals with study was evidently no new thing. S. Benedict did not invent literature or libraries ; he only lent the sanction of his name to the study of the one and the formation of the other. That libraries existed before his period is proved by allusions to them in the Fathers and other early writers ; but, as those allusions are general, and say nothing from which either their size or their arrangement can be inferred, I shall dismiss them in very few sentences. The earliest is said to have been the collection got together at Jerusalem, by Bishop Alexander, at the beginning of the third century. Another was founded about fifty years later at Cæsarea by Origen.

This is described as not only extensive, but remarkable for the importance of the manuscripts it contained. Others are recorded at Hippo, at Cirta, at Constantinople, and at Rome, where both S. Peter's and the Lateran had their special collections of books. I suspect that all these libraries were in connexion with churches, possibly actually within their walls. At Cirta, for example, it is recorded that during the persecution of 303–304 the officers "went to the church where the Christians used to assemble, and spoiled it of chalices, lamps, etc., but when they came into the library (*bibliothecam*), the presses (*armaria*) there were found empty." This language seems to imply that the sacred vessels and the books were in different parts of the same building. The instructions, again, of the dying Augustine, who bequeathed his library to the church at Hippo, lead to the same conclusion. The library of S. Peter's at Rome, though added to the basilica erected by Constantine, long after its primitive foundation, was on the ground-floor in the angle between the nave and the north limb of the transept, a position which may perhaps have been selected in accordance with early usage.

I now pass to the treatment of books in the libraries of the monastic orders. These either adopted the Rule of S. Benedict, or based their own Rule upon its provisions. It will therefore be desirable to examine what he said on the subject of study, and I will translate a few lines from the 48th chapter of his Rule, *Of daily manual labour.*

Idleness is the enemy of the soul; hence brethren ought, at certain seasons, to occupy themselves with manual labour, and again, at certain hours, with holy reading...

Between Easter and the calends of October let them apply themselves to reading from the fourth hour till near the sixth hour. After the sixth hour, when they rise from table, let them rest on their beds in complete silence; or, if any one should wish to read to himself, let him do so in such a way as not to disturb any one else...

From the calends of October to the beginning of Lent let them apply themselves to reading until the second hour... During Lent, let them apply themselves to reading from morning until the end of the third hour...and, in these days of Lent, let them receive a book apiece from the library, and read it straight through. These books are to be given out at the beginning of Lent. It is important that one or two seniors should be appointed to go round the monastery at the hours when brethren are engaged in reading, in case some ill-conditioned brother should be giving himself up to sloth or idle talk, instead of reading steadily; so that not only is he useless to himself, but incites others to do wrong.

"Behold! how great a matter a little fire kindleth!" These simple words, uttered by one who in power of far-reaching influence has had no equal, gave an impulse to study in the ages it once was the fashion to call dark which grew with the growth of the Order—till wherever a Benedictine house arose—or a monastery of any one of the Orders which were but off-shoots from the Benedictine tree—books were multiplied, and a library came into being, small indeed at first, but increasing year by year, till the wealthier houses had gathered together a collection of books that would do credit to a modern University.

It is very interesting to notice, as Order after

Order was founded, a steady development of
feeling with regard to books, and an ever increasing care for their safe-keeping.   S. Benedict
had contented himself with general directions
for study ; the Cluniacs prescribe the selection
of a special officer to take charge of the books,
with an annual audit of them, and the assign-
ment of a single volume to each brother ; the
Carthusians and the Cistercians provide for the
loan of books to extraneous persons under
certain conditions—a provision which the Benedictines in their turn adopted.   Further, by
the time that the Cluniac Customs were drawn
up in the form in which they have come down
to us, it is evident that the number of books
exceeded the number of brethren ; for both in
them, and in the statutes which Lanfranc pro-
mulgated for the use of the English Benedictines in 1070, the keeper of the books is directed
to bring all the books of the House into
Chapter, after which the brethren, one by one,
are to bring in the books they had borrowed

on the same day in the previous year. Some of the former class of books were probably service-books, but, after this deduction has been made, we may fairly conclude that by the end of the eleventh century Benedictine Houses possessed two sets of books: (1) those which were distributed among the brethren ; (2) those which were kept in some safe place, probably the church, as part of the valuables of the House : or, to adopt modern phrases, they had a lending library and a library of reference. The Augustinians go a step farther than the Benedictines and the Orders derived from them, for they prescribe the kind of press in which the books are to be kept. Both they and the Premonstratensians permit their books to be lent on the receipt of a pledge of sufficient value. Lastly, the Friars, though they were established on the principle of holding no possessions of any kind, soon found that books were indispensable ; that, in the words of a Norman Bishop, *Claustrum sine armario, castrum sine armamentario.* So,

C.   2

by a strange irony, it came to pass that their
libraries excelled those of most other Orders, as
Richard de Bury testifies in the *Philobiblon.*

> Whenever we turned aside to the cities and places
> where the Mendicants had their convents...we found
> heaped up amidst the utmost poverty the utmost riches
> of wisdom....
>
> These men are as ants ever preparing their meat in
> the summer, and ingenious bees continually fabricating
> cells of honey... And to pay due regard to truth, although
> they lately at the eleventh hour have entered the Lord's
> vineyard..., they have added more in this brief hour to
> the stock of the sacred books than all the other vine-
> dressers; following in the footsteps of Paul, the last to be
> called but the first in preaching, who spread the gospel of
> Christ more widely than all others.

It might have been expected, from the use
of the word *library* in the Rule of S. Benedict,
that a special room assigned to books would
have been one of the primitive component parts
of every Benedictine House. This, however, is
not the case. Such a room does usually occur
in these Houses, but it will be found, on examination, that it was added to some previously
existing structure in the fourteenth or fifteenth

century. Its absence from the primitive plan brings out two points very clearly : (1) how few books even a wealthy community could afford to possess for several centuries after the foundation of the Order; (2) how strictly the Order adhered to prescribed arrangements in laying out its Houses, for even those built, or rebuilt, after books had become plentiful, do not admit a Library as an indispensable item in their ground-plan.

How then did they bestow their books after they had become too numerous to be kept in the church ? The answer to this question is a very curious one, when we consider what our climate is, and indeed what the climate of the whole of Europe is, during the winter months. The centre of the monastic life was the cloister. Brethren were not allowed to congregate in any other part of the conventual buildings, except when they went into the frater, or dining-hall, for their meals, or at certain hours in certain seasons into the warming-house (*calefactorium*). In the cloister accordingly they kept their books; and there they sat and studied, or conducted the schooling of the novices and choir-boys in winter and in summer alike.

Such a locality as this could not have been very favourable to the preservation of the books themselves. They, however, had a certain amount of protection which was denied to their readers, for they were shut up in presses. The word used for these, *armarium,* is the same as that which was applied by the Romans to their bookcases; and probably the idea of such a piece of furniture was due to a far-off echo of ancient usage. The official who had charge of the books did not derive his name from them, as in modern times, but from the presses which contained them—for he was uniformly styled *armarius.*

As time went on, greater comfort was introduced. The windows of the walk of the cloister where the presses stood, usually the walk next the Church, were glazed—and sometimes not merely with white glass, but with mottoes alluding to the authors whose works were near at hand ; while in some monasteries the elder monks were provided with small wooden studies, called "carrells." A description of the whole system has been preserved for us in that curious book *The Rites of Durham* ; but it must be remembered that this represents the customs of the convent just before the suppression, and therefore gives no idea of the rigour of an earlier time.

Part of the north walk of the cloister, Durham.

In the north syde of the Cloister, from the corner over against the Church dour to the corner over againste the Dorter dour, was all fynely glased from the hight to the sole within a litle of the grownd into the Cloister garth. And in every wyndowe iij Pewes or Carrells, where every one of the old Monks had his carrell, severall by himselfe, that, when they had dyned, they dyd resort to that place of Cloister, and there studyed upon there books, every one in his carrell, all the after nonne, unto evensong tyme. This was there exercise every daie.

All there pewes or carrells was all fynely wainscotted and verie close, all but the forepart, which had carved wourke that gave light in at ther carrell doures of wainscott. And in every carrell was a deske to lye there bookes on. And the carrells was no greater then from one stanchell of the wyndowe to another.

And over against the carrells against the church wall did stande certaine great almeries [or cupbords] of waynscott all full of bookes [with great store of ancient manuscripts to help them in their study], wherein did lye as well the old auncyent written Doctors of the Church as other prophane authors with dyverse other holie mens wourks, so that every one dyd studye what Doctor pleased them best, havinge the Librarie at all tymes to goe studie in besydes there carrells.

No example of an English monastic bookpress has survived, so far as I have been able to discover; but it would be rash to say that none exists. Meanwhile I will shew you a French example of a press, from the sacristy of the Cathedral at Bayeux, but I cannot be sure that it was originally intended to hold books. M. Viollet-Le-Duc, from whom I borrow it, decides that it was probably made early in the thirteenth century.

Cupboard from sacristy of Bayeux Cathedral.

The Durham *Rites* speak only of bookpresses standing in the cloister against the walls;

but it was not unusual to have recesses in the wall itself, fitted with shelves, and probably closed by a door. Two such are to be seen at Worcester, immediately to the north of the chapter-house door. Each is about ten feet wide by two feet deep.

Book-recess, east walk of the cloister, Worcester.

A similar receptacle for books seems to have been contemplated in Augustinian Houses, for in the Customs of the Augustinian Priory of Barnwell, written towards the end of the thirteenth century, the following passage occurs:

The press in which the books are kept ought to be lined inside with wood, that the damp of the walls may not moisten or stain the books. This press should be divided vertically as well as horizontally by sundry partitions, on which the books may be ranged so as to be separated from one another; for fear they be packed so close as to injure each other, or delay those who want them.

Recesses such as these were developed in Cistercian houses into a small square room

without a window, and but little larger than an
ordinary cupboard. In the plans of Clairvaux
and Kirkstall this room is placed between the
chapter-house and the transept of the church ;
and similar rooms, in similar situations, have
been found at Fountains, Beaulieu, Tintern,
Netley, etc. The catalogue, made 1396, of the
Cistercian Abbey at Meaux in Holderness, now
totally destroyed, gives us a glimpse of the
internal arrangement of one of these rooms.
The books were placed on shelves against the
walls, and even over the door. Again, the
catalogue of the House of White Canons at
Titchfield in Hampshire, dated 1400, shews that
the books were kept in a small room, on shelves
there called *columpnæ*, set against the walls. It
is obvious that no study could have gone forward
in such places as these; they must have been
intended for security only, and to replace the
wooden presses used elsewhere.

As time went on, the number of the books
would naturally increase, and by the beginning

of the fifteenth century the larger monasteries at least had accumulated many hundred volumes. For instance, at Christ Church, Canterbury, at the beginning of the 14th century, there were 698. These had to be bestowed in various parts of the House without order or selection,—in presses set up wherever a vacant corner could be found— to the great inconvenience, we may be sure, of the more studious monks, or of scholars who came to consult them. To remedy such a state of things a definite room was constructed for books—in addition to the presses in the cloister, which were still retained for the books in daily use. A few instances of this will suffice. At Christ Church, Canterbury, a library was built between 1414 and 1443 by Archbishop Chichele, over the Prior's Chapel ; at Durham between 1416 and 1446 by Prior Wessyngton, over the old sacristy ; at Citeaux in 1480, over the writing-room (*scriptorium*) ; at Clairvaux between 1495 and 1503, in the same position ; at S. Victor in Paris—an Augustinian House—between 1501 and 1508 ; and at S. Germain des Prés in the same city about 1513, over the south cloister.

Most of us, I take it, have more or less imperfect ideas of the appearance of a great monastery in the days of its completeness ; and information on this point is unfortunately much more defective for our own country than it is for France. In illustration, therefore, of what I have been saying about the position of monastic libraries, I will next shew you two bird's-eye views of the Benedictine House of S. Germain des Prés, Paris. The first, dated 1687, shews the library over the south walk of the cloister, where it was placed in 1513. It must not, however, be supposed that no library existed before this. On the contrary, the House seems to have had one from the first foundation, and so early as the thirteenth century it could be consulted by strangers, and books borrowed from it. The second view, dated 1723, shews a still further extension of the library. It has now invaded the west side of the cloister, which has received

an upper storey, and even the external appearance of the venerable refectory, which was
respected when nearly all the rest of the
buildings were rebuilt in a classical style, has
been sacrificed to a similar gallery.   The united
lengths of these three rooms must have been
little short of 324 feet.   This library was at the
disposal of all scholars who desired to use it.
When the Revolution came it contained more
than 49,000 printed books, and 7000 manuscripts.
The fittings belonged to the period of its latest
extension: they appear to have been sumptuous,
but for my present object, uninteresting.

Views of S. Germain des Prés: (1) *from Frank-
lin, " Anciennes Bibliothèques de Paris,"* i.
126; (2) *from Bouillart, " Histoire de
l'Abbaye de S. Germain des Préz."*

At Canterbury the library, built as I have
said, over the Prior's Chapel, was 60 feet long,
by 22 feet broad ; and we know, from some

memoranda written in 1508, when a number of books were sent to be bound or repaired, that it contained sixteen bookcases, each of which had four shelves. I have calculated that this library could have contained about 2000 volumes.

I have shewn you a Benedictine House, and will next shew you a bird's-eye view of Citeaux, the parent house of the Cistercian Order, founded at the close of the eleventh century. The original was taken, so far as I can make out, about 1500, at any rate before the primitive buildings had been seriously altered. The library here occupied two positions—under the roof between the dormitory and the refectory (which must have been extremely inconvenient); and subsequently it was rebuilt in an isolated situation on the north side of the second cloister, over the writing-room (*scriptorium*). This was also the position of the new library at Clairvaux —the other great Cistercian House in France— the fame of which was equal to, if not greater than, that of Citeaux. Of this latter library we

have two descriptions ; the first written in 1517,
the second in 1723.

*View of Citeaux : from Viollet-Le-Duc, " Diction-
naire de l'Architecture,"* i. 271.

The former account, by the secretary of the
Queen of Sicily, who visited Clairvaux 13 July
1517, is as follows :

> On the same side of the cloister are fourteen studies,
> where the monks write and study, and over the said
> studies is the new library, to which one mounts by a
> broad and lofty spiral staircase from the aforesaid
> cloister. This library is 189 feet long, by 17 feet wide.
> In it are 48 seats (*bancs*), and in each seat 4 shelves
> (*poulpitres*) furnished with books on all subjects, but
> chiefly theology; the greater number of the said books
> are of vellum, and written by hand, richly storied and
> illuminated. The building that contains the said library is
> magnificent, built of stone, and excellently lighted on both
> sides with fine large windows, well glazed, looking out on
> the said cloister and the burial-ground of the brethren...
> The said library is paved throughout with small tiles
> adorned with various designs.

The description written in 1723, by the
learned Benedictines to whom we owe the
Voyage Littéraire, is equally interesting :

From the great cloister you proceed into the cloister of
conversation, so called because the brethren are allowed
to converse there.   In this cloister there are 12 or 15
little cells, all of a row, where the brethren formerly used
to write books; for this reason they are still called at the
present day the writing-rooms.   Over these cells is the
Library, the building for which is large, vaulted, well
lighted, and stocked with a large number of manuscripts,
fastened by chains to desks; but there are not many
printed books.

In the great cloister, on the side next the
Chapter House, the same observer noted "books
chained on wooden desks, which brethren can
come and read when they please."   The library
was for serious study, the cloister for daily
reading, probably in the main devotional.

If my time were unlimited I could describe
to you several other fifteenth century monastic
libraries, but I feel that I must content myself
with only one more—that of the Franciscan
House in London, commonly called Christ's
Hospital.   The first stone of this library was
laid by Sir Richard Whittington, 21 October,
1421, and by Christmas Day in the following

year the roof was finished. Stow tells us that
it was 129 feet long by 31 feet broad ; and the
Letters Patent of Henry the Eighth add that it
had 28 desks, and 28 double settles of wainscot.
The whole building—so well worth preservation
—has been totally destroyed, but I am able to
shew you a view of it.

*Library of Christ's Hospital: from Trollope's
"History of Christ's Hospital,"* p. 105.

This view is an excellent illustration of the
point on which I have insisted, namely, that in
the course of the fifteenth century the great
religious Houses—no matter to what Order they
belonged—found that their books had become
too numerous for the localities primitively intended for them, and began to build special
libraries—usually over some existing structure ;
or—in other words—established a library of
reference, which was not unfrequently thrown
open to scholars in general, who were allowed
to borrow books from it, on execution of an

indenture, or deposit of a sufficient pledge. " It
is safer to fall back on a pledge, than to proceed
against an individual," said the Customs of the
Priory at Abingdon.

In what way were these monastic libraries
fitted up ? No trace of any monastic fittings
has survived, so far as I am aware, either in
England, or in France, or in Italy ; and even
M. Viollet-Le-Duc dismisses " The Library " in
a few brief sentences, of which the keynote is
despair. My own view is that a close analogy
may be traced between the fittings of monastic
libraries and those of collegiate libraries ; and
that when we understand the one we shall
understand the other.

The collegiate system was in no sense of
the word monastic, indeed it was to a certain
extent established to counteract monastic influence ; but it is absurd to suppose that the
younger communities would borrow nothing
from the elder—especially when we reflect that
the monastic system had completed at least

seven centuries of successful existence before Walter de Merton was moved to found a college; that many of the subsequent founders of colleges were churchmen, if not actually monks; and that there were monastic colleges at both Universities. Further, as we have seen that study was specially enjoined upon the monks by S. Benedict, it is precisely in the direction of study that we should expect to find common features in the two sets of communities. And this, in fact, is what came to pass. An examination of the statutes affecting the library in the codes imposed upon the colleges of Oxford and Cambridge shews that their provisions were borrowed directly from the monastic Customs. The resemblances are too striking to be accidental. Take, for instance, this clause, from the statutes of Oriel College, Oxford, dated 1329:

The common books (*communes libri*) of the House are to be brought out and inspected once a year, on the feast of the Commemoration of Souls [2 November], in pre-

C.   3

sence of the Provost or his deputy, and of the Scholars
[Fellows].

Every one of them in turn, in order of seniority, may
select a single book which either treats of the science to
which he is devoting himself, or which he requires for his
use. This he may keep until the same festival in the
succeeding year, when a similar selection of books is to
take place, and so on, from year to year. If there should
happen to be more books than persons, those that remain
are to be selected in the same manner.

Bishop Bateman—who had been educated in
the priory at Norwich, and whose brother was
an abbot—gave statutes to Trinity Hall, Cambridge, in 1350, with similar provisions, and the
addition that certain books "are to remain con-
tinuously in the library-chamber, fastened with
iron chains, for the common use of the Fellows."
These were copied by Wykeham at New College,
Oxford, but with extended provisions for lending
books to students, and a direction that all the
books "which remain unassigned after the
Fellows have made their selection are to be
fastened with iron chains, and remain for ever
in the common Library." This statute was

repeated at King's College, Cambridge, and at several colleges in Oxford.

Let me now remind you of Archbishop Lanfranc's statute for English Benedictines, dated 1070, which was based, as he himself tells us, on the general monastic practice of his time :

On the Monday after the first Sunday in Lent, before brethren come into the Chapter House, the librarian (*custos librorum*) shall have had a carpet laid down, and all the books got together upon it, except those which a year previously had been assigned for reading. These brethren are to bring with them, when they come into the Chapter House, each his book in his hand....

Then the librarian shall read a statement as to the manner in which brethren have had books during the past year. As each brother hears his name pronounced he is to give back the book which had been entrusted to him for reading; and he whose conscience accuses him of not having read the book through which he had received, is to fall on his face, confess his fault, and entreat forgiveness.

The librarian shall then make a fresh distribution of books, namely, a different volume to each brother for his reading.

You will agree with me, I feel sure, that this statute, or similar provisions extracted from

other regulations, is the source of the collegiate
provisions for an annual audit and distribution
of books ; while the reservation of the undis-
tributed volumes, and their chaining for common
use in a library, was in accordance with the
unwritten practice of the monasteries.   This
being the case I think that we are justified in
assuming that the internal fittings of the libraries
would be identical also ; and it must be further
remembered that both collegiate and monastic
libraries were being fitted up during the same
period, the fifteenth century.

When books were first placed in a separate
room, fastened with iron chains, for the use of
the Fellows of a college or the monks of a
convent, the piece of furniture used was, I take
it, an elongated lectern or desk, of a convenient
height for a seated reader to use.   The books
lay on their sides on the desk, and were attached
by chains to a horizontal bar above it.   There
were at least two libraries in this University
fitted with such desks, at the colleges of Pem-

broke and Queens'; and that it was a common
form abroad is proved by its appearance in a
French translation of the first book of the

FIG. I.   Interior of a library: from a MS. of a French translation of the first book
of the *Consolations of Philosophy* of Boethius.

Consolations of Philosophy of Boethius, which I lately found in the British Museum[1], executed towards the end of the fifteenth century (fig. 1).

One example at least of these fittings still exists, in the library attached to the church of S. Wallberg, at Zutphen in Holland. This library was built in its present position in 1555, but I suspect that some of the fittings, those namely which are more richly ornamented, were removed from an earlier library. Each of these desks is 9 feet long by 5 feet 6 inches high ; and, as you will see directly, a man can sit and read at them very conveniently. I shall shew you first a general view of part of the library (fig. 2) ; and, secondly, a single desk (fig. 3).

Such cases as these must have been in use at the Sorbonne, where a library was first established in 1289 for books chained for the common convenience of the Fellows (*in communem sociorum utilitatem*). A description of this library, based probably on records now lost,

[1] MSS. Harl. 4335.

has been given by Claude Hémeré (Librarian 1638—1643) in his MS. history.   This I proceed to translate :

FIG. 3.   Desk in the library at Zutphen : from a photograph.

The old library was contained under one roof.   It was firmly and solidly built, and was 120 feet long by 36 feet broad.   Further, that it might be the more safe from the danger of being burnt, should any house in the neighbourhood catch fire, there was a sufficient interval between it and every dwelling-house. Each side was pierced with 19 windows of equal size, that plenty of daylight both from the east and the west (for this was the direction of the room) might fall upon the desks, and fill the whole length and breadth of the library. There were 28 desks, marked with the letters of the alphabet, five feet high, and so arranged that they were separated by a moderate interval. They were loaded with books, all of which were chained, that no sacrilegious hand might [carry them off. These chains were attached to the right-hand board of every book] so that they might be readily thrown aside, and reading not be interfered with. Moreover the volumes could be opened and shut without difficulty. A reader who sat down in the space between two desks, as they rose to a height of five feet as I said above, neither saw nor disturbed any one else who might be reading or writing in another place by talking or by any other interruption, unless the other student wished it, or paid attention to any question that might be put to him. It was required, by the ancient rules of the library, that reading, writing, and handling of books should go forward in complete silence.

This system must have been very wasteful as regards space ; for only a few volumes, say a couple of dozen, could be accommodated on a single desk. As books accumulated therefore some other form of case had to be devised, which would accommodate more volumes than could be consulted at once. The desk could not be dispensed with so long as books were chained, but one or more shelves were added to it. This addition was effected in two ways, according as the books were to stand on their ends, or to lie on their sides.

As an illustration of the former plan I will take the library of Merton College, Oxford, attributed by tradition to William Reade, Bishop of Chichester 1368—85 ; and it has been so little altered that it may be taken as a type of a medieval collegiate or monastic library. It is a long narrow room, as all medieval libraries were, with equidistant windows, and the book-cases stand at right angles to the walls in the spaces between each pair of windows, in front of which is the seat for the reader. Each book-case had originally two shelves only above the desk. I will shew you, first, a general view of the interior of this library, and then a single bookcase and seat.

Merton College, Oxford: (1) *general view of the interior of the Library;* (2) *a single bookcase as at present.*

The system of chaining, as adopted in this country, would allow of the books being readily taken down from the shelves, and laid on the desk for reading. One end of the chain was attached to the middle of the upper edge of the right-hand board; the other to a ring which played on a bar set in front of the shelf on which the book stood. The fore-edge of the books, not the back, was turned forwards. A swivel, usually in the middle of the chain, prevented tangling. The chains varied in length according to the distance of the shelf from the desk. The bar was kept in place by a rather elaborate system of iron-work attached to the end of the bookcase, and secured by a lock which often required two keys—that is, the presence of two officials—to open it. To illustrate this I will shew you a sketch of

one of the bookcases in Hereford Cathedral
(fig. 4).

FIG. 4. Bookcase in Hereford Cathedral. (Lent by
the Syndics of the University Press.)

Having said thus much about chaining, I
return to the Merton bookcases. Cases similar
to these were evidently in use in the library
of Christ Church, Canterbury, where the memoranda I mentioned record four shelves—
that is, two on each side—in each bookcase,
and also at Clairvaux, where a similar feature

was observed.   The design was evidently much admired, for we find cases on a similar plan, but larger, elsewhere in Oxford, as at the Colleges of Corpus Christi, S. John's, Trinity, Jesus, and in the Bodleian Library.

Bookcase in the Library of Corpus Christi College, Oxford.

Another device for combining desk with shelf is to be seen at Trinity Hall, Cambridge, and, as these cases were set up after 1626, we have here a curious instance of a deliberate return to ancient forms.   There is evidence that there once existed below the shelf a second desk, which could be drawn in and out as required, so that a reader could stand or sit as he pleased, as you will see from the next illustration.

Bookcase in the Library of Trinity Hall, Cambridge.

The University of Leiden in Holland adopted a modification of this design, for there the shelf

is above the desk, and readers could only stand
to use the books (fig. 5).

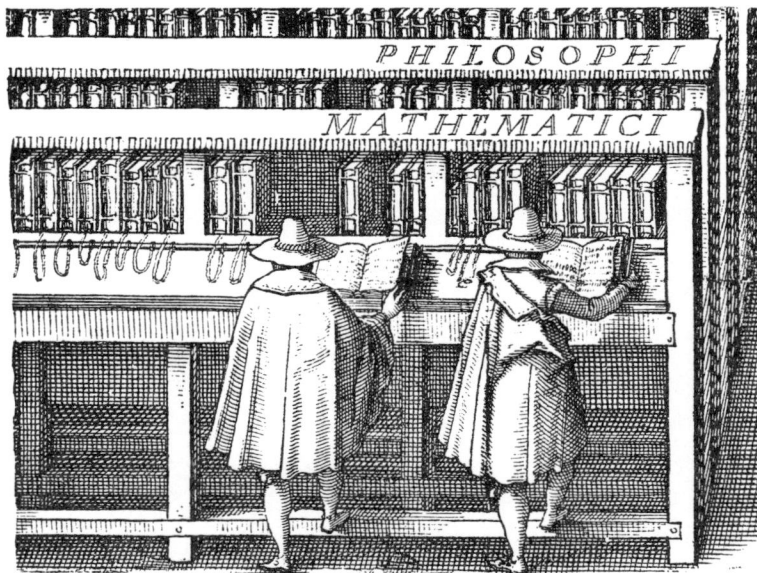

FIG. 5. Bookcases in the library of the University of Leiden : from a print by
J. C. Woudanus, dated 1610. (Lent by the Syndics of the University Press.)

An arrangement analogous to this was
adopted at Citeaux, as we may gather from the
catalogue, drawn up in 1480. I will not trouble

you with details, but merely say that there was evidently a shelf below the desk as well as one above it. The cases therefore resembled those at Leiden, with this difference ; and they were also probably of such a height that a reader could conveniently sit at them.

On the continent, where elaborate bindings came early into fashion, sometimes protected by equally elaborate bosses at their corners, it would have been impossible to arrange the volumes as we did side by side on the shelves. It therefore became the fashion to place a shelf below the desk, and to lay the books upon it on their sides. The earliest library fitted in this manner that I have been able to discover is at Cesena in North Italy. It was built in 1452, by Domenico Malatesta Novello, for the convent of S. Francesco. It is possible, therefore, that the parent house of S. Francesco at Assisi, which had a large library, divided, so early as 1381, into a *Libreria publica* and a *Libreria secreta*, had similar bookcases. I am going to shew you a general view of the room, which has a thoroughly medieval character, next the cases (fig. 6), and thirdly a single book with its chain (fig. 7). You will observe that the seats for the reader are no longer independent, but are combined with the bookcase.

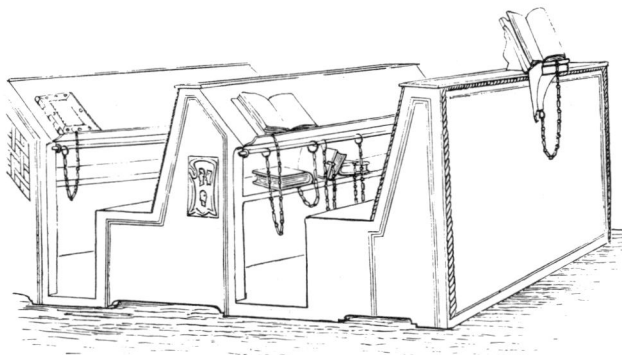

FIG. 6. Bookcases at west end of south side of Library, Cesena.

These cases no doubt suggested those in the Medicean library at Florence, begun in 1525 by Michael Angelo. The cases, perhaps the finest specimens in existence of wood-carving as applied to this style of work, were designed by other artists shortly after the completion of the room.

FIG. 7.   Part of a single bookcase in the Library, Cesena.

Bookcase in the Medicean Library at Florence.

In English libraries at least bookcases arranged on what I may term the Oxford type were in general use throughout the sixteenth and seventeenth centuries. The invention of printing had largely increased the number of volumes, and at the same time diminished their value, so that chaining was no longer necessary. When it had been abandoned neither a desk, nor a seat in close proximity to the books, was required. In consequence, though libraries continued to be built on the ancient type with numerous windows close to the floor, it was possible to alter the old cases, or to make new ones, with a far larger number of shelves than heretofore ; and when further space for books was needed, low cases were interposed between each pair of tall ones. A splendid specimen of this treatment is to be seen at S. John's College, Cambridge, where the bookcases were put up soon after the completion of the library in 1628.

C.   4

Though the plinth and central pilaster have been taken away, and the levels of the shelves changed, their original appearance can be recovered at a glance. On the top of all the low cases there was a desk, in memory of that of ancient times. At the end of the taller cases is a panel to contain the catalogue, here closed by a small door.

Bookcases in S. John's College Library.

Sometimes, as we see at Peterhouse, ancient usage asserted itself so far that a seat was contrived by making the plinth of the tall case project to a sufficient distance. These book-cases were set up between 1641 and 1648.

Bookcase in Peterhouse Library.

When the necessity for still further space for books became imperative, the seat was given up, or was dropped to the height of a step, as in the bookcases in the south room of the University

Library, Cambridge, put up soon after 1649. The carved wing, however, which had masked the ends of it, was retained as an ornament, both there and in the old library at Pembroke College, Cambridge, furnished soon after 1690.

Meanwhile a new system of arranging book-cases had come into use on the continent. So far as I have been able to discover, the first library arranged in the way with which we are familiar, namely, with the bookcases set against the walls instead of at right angles to them, is that of the Escurial. These cases were made by Herrera, the architect of the building, in 1584. There is no indication of chaining, but, in con-formity with ancient usage, the fore edge of the books, instead of their backs, is turned outwards, and the desk is represented by a shelf, carried all round the room at a convenient height. No doubt so important a structure as this, erected by so mighty a potentate as the King of Spain, would be much talked about, and provoke imitators. Among these, I feel sure, was Cardinal

4—2

Mazarin, whose library was fitted up in Paris in or about 1647, as a library to be used daily by the public. After his death his books and bookcases were moved to the building in which they may still be seen. I will now shew you views of the two libraries, and you shall decide whether it is not obvious that the one was suggested by the other.

Interior of the Library of the Escurial and of the Bibliothèque Mazarine, Paris.

The new system was not accepted hastily. I believe that Sir Christopher Wren, when he built Trinity College Library in 1695, was the first English architect who ventured to build a library with windows which, as he says himself, "rise high, and give place for the deskes against the walls." I suspect that he borrowed this latter idea from France, which he visited in 1665, and most likely from the Bibliothèque Mazarine, for he has himself recorded his admiration for "the masculine furniture of the Palais Mazarin," though he does not specially mention the library. But he did not discard the ancient arrangement alto-gether. On the contrary he utilised it so far as to subdivide the room, and provide recesses for the convenience of students. He says:

The disposition of the shelves both along the walls and breaking out from the walls must needes prove very convenient and gracefull, and the best way for the students will be to have a litle square table in each celle with 2 chaires. The necessity of bringing windowes and dores to answer to the old building leaves two squarer places at the endes, and 4 lesser celles not to study in, but to be shut up with some neat lattice dores for archives.

One compartment of Trinity College Library.

I need hardly say that neither this library, nor any of those built by Wren's pupils or imitators, shew traces of chaining. The old fashion, however, lingered. In 1651 Humphrey Cheetham directed the books he gave to certain specified parish-churches near Manchester to be chained; in 1694 James Leaver gave books to the grammar-school at Bolton in Lancashire which were chained in a cupboard very like the *armarium* of a monastic cloister ;

Book-cupboard and desk at Bolton, Lancashire.
The former is lettered: " The gift of Mr
James Leaver, citison of London 1694."

and at All Saints Church, Hereford, a collection of books bequeathed in 1715 was chained to ordinary shelves set against the walls, as may still be seen. This very obvious way of disposing of books evidently shocked old-fashioned people, for Cole the antiquary, writing in 1703, could still speak of the arrangement of shelves against the walls as *à la moderne*.

The libraries I have been describing were more or less public, and I should like, before I conclude, to shew you how books were bestowed in the studies of individual scholars—whether royal, monastic, or secular.

I conceive that for many centuries after the beginning of the Christian era the methods of the

ancient world were followed; and that private
libraries were arranged upon the Roman model
in presses, with busts, mottoes, and the like.
Such was the library of Isidore, Bishop of
Seville (601–636). He was a voluminous writer,
and seems to have had a voluminous library,
divided, if I interpret the arrangements correctly,
among fourteen presses, each ornamented by
one or more portrait-busts or medallions with
suitable verses beneath them. The series con-
cludes with a notice *Ad interventorem*, a person
whom we may call *A talkative intruder* :

> Non patitur quenquam coram se scriba loquentem :
> Non est hic quod agas, garrule, perge foras.

How useful such an admonition would be in
modern libraries, if only it could be enforced !

So late as the end of the twelfth century I
find a Bishop who bequeathed his library to a
church describing it as "the contents of my
press (*plenarium armarium meum*)."

Gradually, however, other methods came

into fashion, due probably to the introduction of the handsome bindings of which I have already spoken. Some particulars have fortunately been preserved of the cost of fitting up a certain tower in the Louvre between 1364 and 1368, to contain the books belonging to Charles the Fifth of France, from which much useful information may be extracted. The fittings of the older library in the palace on the Isle de la Cité were to be taken down and altered, and set up in the new room. Two carpenters are paid for "having taken to pieces all the cases (*bancs*) and two wheels (*roes*), that is revolving desks, which were in the king's library in the palace, and transported them to the Louvre... ; and for having put all together again, and hung up the cases (*lettrins*) in the two upper stages of the tower that looks toward the Falconry, to put the king's books in ; and for having panelled ... the first of those two stories all round inside." Next a wire-worker (*cagetier*) is paid "for having made trellises of wire in front of two casements and two windows ... to keep out birds and other beasts (*oyseaux et autres bestes*) by reason of, and protection for, the books that shall be placed there."

The words *bancs* and *lettrins*, which I have translated "cases," are both frequently used. The first commonly denotes the cases in monastic libraries, and the second is the usual word for a reading-desk. I think, therefore, that the two words were applied to describe the same piece of furniture, as "stall" and "desk" were with us. I am now going to shew you two pictures of rooms arranged for study, which fit the above description very well. The first is from a French translation of Boccaccio, *Des cas des maleureux nobles hommes et femmes*, written and illuminated in Flanders for King Henry the Seventh[1]. Two gentlemen are studying at a revolving desk, which can be raised or lowered by a screw. This is evidently the "wheel" of the French king's library. Behind are their books, either

[1] *MSS. Mus. Brit.* 14. E. v.

resting on a desk hung against the wall (which is panelled), or lying on a shelf beneath the desk.   The second is also Flemish, of the same date, from a copy of the *Miroir historial*[1]. It represents a monk, probably the author of the book, writing in his study.   Behind him are three desks, one above the other, hung against the wall, with books, as in the first picture, resting upon them.

Some such arrangement as this must have been long in fashion.   Libraries such as those of Diane de Poitiers and Francis the First could not have been bestowed in any other way; and in fact, when books are enriched with metal-work, or have specially elaborate ornaments on their sides, a desk of some sort is indispensable.

Humbler scholars had to content themselves with small cupboards constructed in the thickness of the wall, or hung against it, as in the picture I will next shew you, from a French translation of Valerius Maximus, copied for

[1] *MSS. Mus. Brit.* 14. E. 1.

King Edward the Fourth, and dated 1479[1]. You will observe that the lower part of the window is fitted with trellises as in the French king's library, not casements. The upper part only is glazed.

Another, and apparently very usual way of bestowing books, especially when they were not numerous, was to place them in a sort of cupboard under the sloping desk on which the owner read or wrote. An excellent specimen of this device—which Richard de Bury specially commends, as being modelled on the Ark, in the side of which the book of the Law was put—is to be found in the *Ship of Fools* (1498). Another, of a curiously modern type, occurs in an *Hours* in the Fitzwilliam Museum, Cambridge, executed about 1445 for Isabel, Duchess of Brittany.

Sometimes this book-cupboard supported a revolving desk, which could be raised or depressed by the help of a central screw—like those I shewed you just now ; sometimes

[1] *MSS. Mus. Brit.* 18. E. IV.

the desk alone appears, with books laid on it. The forms given to these pieces of furniture by the ingenuity of those who made them are infinite ; and they often include beautiful designs for armchairs, fitted with desks for writing. I will shew you just one—not because it is specially beautiful, but because it gives a quaint picture of a scholar's room at the beginning of the fifteenth century[1].

Here Time—as represented by yonder clock —holds up his finger and bids me stop. I would fain have shewn you more pictures—but I hope that you have seen a sufficient number to give you some idea of the surroundings in which our forefathers read and wrote. I am sure that only in this way can we realise that they were real living people—not mere names. Their modes of thought were far different from ours ; they may have wasted their time in verbal subtleties, and uncritical tales ; but the more we study what they did, the more we shall

[1] *MSS. Mus. Brit.* 20. B. xx.

realise how laborious, how artistic, how conscientious they were; and amid all the developments of the nineteenth century, we shall gratefully confess that the Middle Ages rocked the cradle of our knowledge, and that we "See but their hope become reality."

ILLUSTRATIONS.

1. Interior of a library, from Boethius.

2. General view of part of the library attached to the Church of S. Wallberg at Zutphen.

3. Desk in the library at Zutphen.

4. Bookcase in Hereford Cathedral.

5. Bookcases in the library of the University of Leiden.

6. Bookcases at west end of south side of library, Cesena.

7. Part of a single bookcase in the library, Cesena.

1969

BIBLIOTHECA ARGONAUTICA

CATALOGUE OF SCHOLARLY BOOKS
IN THE FIELDS OF

MEDIAEVAL STUDIES

BYZANTIUM

AMERICANA

HISTORY AND NUMISMATICS

ARGONAUT INC., PUBLISHERS
737 North Michigan Avenue
Chicago, Illinois 60611

ESSAYS ON THE LATIN ORIENT. W. Miller. viii + 582 pp. + 9 plates + 1 map $18.25

The best study of the relations between Europe and the Near East during the Crusades. Reprint of the 1921 edition. (D—)

HISTOIRE DU COMMERCE DU LEVANT AU MOYEN ÂGE. W. Heyd. Royal octavo. 2 Vols. xxiv + 554 pp. & 799 pp. $45.00

Reprint of the Leipzig 1885-86 edition. The best work on trade in the East and Near East during the medieval period. (D—)

TRAITÉ DE NUMISMATIQUE DU MOYEN ÂGE. A. Engel & R. Serrure. 3 Vols.* lxxxvii + 1459 pp., illus. $65.00

Reprint of the unique reference work (1891-1905) for the study ot medieval monetary history and numismatics.

This work is for the medievalist what Barclay V. Head's *Historia Numorum* is to students of Greek coins.

A standard reference library volume, with illustrations of 1972 coins. (D—)

ANTIQUITATES ITALICAE MEDII AEVI. L. Muratori. 6 Vols. 3747 pp., illus. 8½ x 11. $165.00

Reprint of the most rare reference work on medieval Italy (1738-42). The texts collected and the subjects illustrated herein combine to create a complete encyclopaedia of public and private life of the times with much information seldom available from other sources. Language, government, laws, magistrates, costume, trade, scholarship, arts and letters, military life, weapons, money and coins and other aspects of medieval Italian life are fully documented in this unique work necessary to any college or university library or the medievalist. (D—)

DIZIONARIO ARALDICO. P. Guelfi Camajani. 585 pp., illus. + 2 color plates $7.00

An heraldic dictionary with 573 text illustrations including crests, symbols, mottoes and other information. Valuable for heraldists, historians and art students. (D—)

MOTTI ARALDICI EDITI DI FAMIGLIE ITALIANE. U. Dallari. 221 pp.* $7.00

An alphabetical listing of 2745 mottos from the crests of Italian families interpreted for students of art, heraldry, numismatics and the history of medieval Italy. (D—)

REGENTEN-TABELLEN. Max Wilberg. Royal Octavo. viii + 336 $15.00

A unique volume of tables of dynasties, royal and noble families of every nation from antiquity to the beginning of the twentieth century. Arranged by country with dates of reigns. Reprint of 1906 edition. An indispensable work for reference libraries, historians and numismatists. (D—)

THE BIRDS OF SHAKESPEARE. James Edmund Harting. With Prolegomena by Grundy Steiner. 360 pp., illus. LC 65-15462. $7.50

First published in 1871 this book remains a favorite among bird lovers and Shakespeare aficionados alike. A work of careful scholarship, it examines Shakespeare's many references to birds and explains the ornithological terminology used by the Bard in light of what he must have known about natural history. "No book about either ornithology or Shakespeare is more enjoyable than this one." *Texas Parks and Wildlife*. (D—)

THE ART AND SPORT OF FALCONRY. George Kotsiopoulos. 128 pp. LC 65-15463. $6.00

Three original translations of medieval manuscripts on falconry, with an introduction by the editor on falconry in America today. The three texts translated are *The Book of King Dancus, Treatise on Falconry* by Albertus Magnus, and a fragment from a Franco-Norman falconry handbook. These describe the care and training of falcons and their use in the "hunt." This book is of ornithological, historical and literary importance. (D 3)

ORTSNAMEN GRIECHENLANDS IN "FRANKISCHER" ZEIT. Otto Markl. 66 pp. + 2 plates* $3.00

Actually a geographic dictionary of "Frankish" and "Venetian" Greece, this 1966 publication, including almost all known place names in use during the period covered, becomes a major sourcebook for the student of history and historical geography. With an excellent bibliography to which all entries are referred. Important for geographical and historical libraries. (B—)

COINAGE IN THE BALKANS 820 — 1355. D. M. Metcalf. xix + 286 + 16 plates. LC 66-20439. $10.00

A major new reference book illuminating the economic history and the coinages of the Balkan peninsula during one of the least well known historical periods. The author examines trade routes, provincial coinage, mints and their issues, Imperial Byzantine economic policy, the inflation of coinage, etc. with maps and charts. Invaluable for collectors of the Byzantine series and all students of this period of history. (D—)

MEDIEVAL BRACTEATES: AN EMPIRICAL GUIDE. J. F. Lhotka, Jr. 48 pp., illus.* $2.00

An identification guide with a list of inscriptions and a systematic analysis of the types in this important group of medieval Germanic coins. Bibliography. (A—)

MEDIEVAL FEUDAL FRENCH COINAGE. J. H. Lhotka, Jr. 36 pp., illus.* $1.50

The unique introduction, in English, to this historically interesting coin series. (A—)

THE COINAGE OF SOUTH GERMANY IN THE THIRTEENTH CENTURY. D. M. Metcalf. 79 pp., illus., maps. $4.00

The theme of this monograph is the influence of the geographical setting on the issue and circulation of coinage in 13th century South Germany and the increasing localization of issues connected with the growth in size of the main towns. 718 coins catalogued. (A—)

BIBLIOGRAFIA NUMISMATICA MEDIOEVALE ITALIANA. R. Ciferro. 498 pp.* $5.00

An extensive bibliography published in 1961 for the historian or numismatist working with medieval Italian coinage. (D—)

SURVEY OF MEDIEVAL IBERIAN COINAGES. J. F. Lhotka, Jr. and **P. K. Anderson.** 123 pp., illus.* $5.00

An excellent introduction to the coinage and monetary history of medieval Spain. With excellent lists of inscriptions, dynastic tables and analyses of portraits, symbols and scenes appearing as coin types. (A—)

LE MONETE DI VENEZIA. N. Papadopoli Aldobrandini. 4 Vols. 2382 pp. + 150 plates* $80.00

Reprint of the basic reference work (1893-1919) on the coins of the Venetian democracy. Remains the basic guide to Venetian coins and a unique source for material on the economic history of Venice. (D 2)

CORPUS DER MITTELALTERLICHEN MÜNZEN VON KROATIEN, SLAVONIEN, DALMATIEN UND BOSNIEN. Ivan Rengjeo. Quarto. 142 pp. + 26 plates* $12.00

A corpus of all known types of medieval coins from Croatia, Slavonia, Dalmatia and Bosnia collected for the first time. Extremely important for the study of medieval central Europe and the Balkans in history and numismatics. (D—)

CORPUS NUMMORUM HUNGARIAE. Ladislaus Rethy and **Gunther Probszt.** 132 pp. + 49 plates $16.00

The unique reference for medieval coins of Hungary. Valuable source material for historians and economists. (D—)

NUMISMATIQUE DE L'ORIENT LATIN. G. Schlumberger. 506 + 38 suppl. + 22 plates, map. $50.00

A reprint of the unique reference work to date on the coinages of the Crusaders and the Frankish East. Necessary and invaluable for all reference libraries on medieval art, numismatics and history. (D—)

MONETE INEDITE DEI GRAN MAESTRI DELL ORDINE DI S. GIOVANNI IN RODI. P. Lambros. 36 + 20 pp. + 2 plates* $4.00

The unique reference for the coinage of the knights of St. John of Jerusalem issued on the island of Rhodes (1291-1523). Reprint of the 1865 edition. (D 2)

THE COINS OF THE GENOVESE RULERS OF CHIOS (1314-1329). Paul Lambros. 30 pp. + 2 plates $2.00

The first translation from the Greek original (1885) which is the unique treatise on the coins used under Benedict and Martinus Zacharias, rulers of the island of Chios. (D 4)

MONNAIES INÉDITES DU ROYAUME DE CHYPRE AU MOYEN ÂGE. P. Lambros. 115 pp. + 9 plates* $5.00

Reprint of the most rare work on Cypriote medieval coinage. Many rare coins appear only in this book which includes the original Greek text (1876) and its French translation. (D 2)

CATALOGUE DES MONNAIES TURCOMANES. I. Khalil Edhem. xvii + 175 pp. + 8 plates* $7.00

The best catalogue available of the coins and coinage of the three primary Turcoman dynasties which ruled from 1090-1231 A.D. Unique sources for the historian. Reprint. (D—)

CATALOGUE DES MONNAIES RUSSES de tous les Princes, Tsars et Empereurs depuis 980 jusqu'a 1899. V. I. Petrov. Quarto. 90 pp. + 46 plates. $15.00
  Reprint of the famous 1899 edition of an unusually complete catalogue, with text in French and Russian. (D—)

THE SILVER COINAGE OF IMPERIAL RUSSIA 1682 - 1917. H. M. Severin.
276 + 48 plates.   **$15.50**
  A definitive reference tool assembling numerous Russian and non-Russian source materials of the past 60 years on all silver denominations from kopeck through 2-ruble pieces of the Imperial period. Over 4200 coins catalogued with appendices of weights, name translations, etc. (A—)

COINS OF THE URTUKI TURKUMANS. FOES OF THE CRUSADERS 1148–1293. STANLEY L.
POOLE. A catalogue of the coins of the Urtukis of Syria, one of the few Moslem dynasties to introduce images on their coins ... but not their own. Reprint of the 1875 edition. *xii + 44 pages, 7 plates*   *$ 6.00*

THE COINS OF THE AMAWI KHALIFEHS. STAN-
LEY LANE POOLE. The coins of the Amawi Khalifehs were the first purely Mohammedan coins issued by the Arabs. They provide a strong contrast to the coins of the early Muslim world and Byzantium. A fundamental monograph based on the collection of Colonel Seton Guthrie. A reprint of the 1874 edition. *x + 38 pages, 5 plates   paper covers*   *$ 4.00*

CATALOGUE OF ORIENTAL COINS IN THE BRITISH MUSEUM. Stanley Lane-Poole; R. S. Poole, editor. 10 Vols. Royal octavo. London 1875-1890. (Reprint) (D3). Separate volumes $30.00 each. Set complete. $250.00
  Vol. 1 *The coins of the Eastern Khaleefehs* (1875), 263 pp. + 8 plates
  Vol. 2 *The coins of the Mohammadan dynasties* (1876), 279 pp. + 8 plates
  Vol. 3 *The coins of the Turkuman houses of Seljook, Urtuk, Zengee* (1877), 305 pp. + 12 plates
  Vol. 4 *The coinage of Egypt:* A.H. 358-922 (1879), 279 pp. + 8 plates
  Vol. 5 *Coins of the Moors of Africa and Spain* (1880), 175 pp. + 7 plates
  Vol. 6 *The coins of the Mongols* (1881) 300 pp. + 9 plates
  Vol. 7 *The coinage of Bukhara (Transoxiana)* (1882), 131 pp. + 5 plates
  Vol. 8 *The coins of the Turcs* (1883), 431 pp. + 12 plates
  Vols. 9-10 *Additions* (1889-1890)

CATALOGUE OF THE COLLECTION OF ORIENTAL COINS OF SETON GUTHRIE. Stanley Lane-Poole. viii + 38 pp. + 5 plates $4.00

THE RUSSIAN MONETARY SYSTEM. I.G.SPASS-
KY. Translated by Z.I. Gorishina and revised by L. Forrer. The first book in English to describe the monetary system and coins of Russia, giving the background of the various issues from earliest (pre-Mongol) times to the latest Soviet pieces. There are also chapters on the various economic reforms and on the significance of the Russian monetary system in world economy through the ages. *253 pages, 212 text illustrations   8½ x 11 $ 20.00*

CHU-FAN-CHI: OR CHINESE AND ARAB TRADE IN THE XIIth and XIIIth CENTURIES. Chau Ju-Kua. Translated and annotated in English by **W. W. Rockhill** and **F. Hirth.** x + 288 + 72 pp. + folding map. $15.00
    The very important text of the Chinese author who remains our main source of information on the Arab-controlled trade of the West with the Chinese Empire in the Middle-Ages. A volume absolutely necessary for any library or scholar interested in the relations of the medieval world with the Far East. Reprint of the 1911-14 edition. (A 3)

THE ART AND SPORT OF FALCONRY. George Kotsiopoulos. 128 pp. LC 65-15463. $6.00

Three original translations of medieval manuscripts on falconry, with an introduction by the editor on falconry in America today. The three texts translated are *The Book of King Dancus, Treatise on Falconry* by Albertus Magnus, and a fragment from a Franco-Norman falconry handbook. These describe the care and training of falcons and their use in the "hunt." This book is of ornithological, historical and literary importance. (D 3)

THE CHRONICLE OF MOREA

JOHN SCHMITT, editor

A political history in verse, relating the establishment of feudalism in Greece by the Franks in the thirteenth century. This is the best reference edition of this important historical text, edited from the manuscripts of Copenhagen and Paris (parallel texts) with an introduction, critical notes and indices. Reprint of the 1904 edition.

xcii + 640 pp. + 1 map **$ 30.00**

ANTIQUITÉS RUSSES. Societe royale des antiquaires du nord, editors, with a preface by **Carl Christian Rafn.** 2 Vols. Folio 1035 pp. + 23 plates, some in color $100.00

An extremely interesting sourcebook, reprinted from the edition of 1850-52, for those interested in ancient Russian history. It includes all the ancient Icelandic and Scandinavian texts in the original languages, with Latin translations, referring to early Russia. Includes commentaries, notes and genealogical tables. (A 2)

ANCIENT ARMOUR AND WEAPONS IN EUROPE

JOHN HEWITT

The most complete history of European armour and weapons from the dawn of the Iron Age in the north to the end of the seventeenth century. This important reference set is a mine of useful information derived from documentary, literary and iconographic sources and a work of great erudition. Reprint of the 1855-1860 edition.

3 Volumes 1228 pp. + 232 plates **$ 50.00**

MÜNZGESCHICHTE DER SCHWEIZ. L. Coraggioni. xi + 184 pp. + 50 plates* $32.00

Reprint of the basic reference work (1896) for the study of medieval, Renaissance and modern (through the 19th century) coins of Switzerland. (D 3)

MANUEL DE BIBLIOGRAPHIE HISTORIQUE. Ch. Victor-Langlois. 2 Vols., bound in 1, 636 pp. $16.00

A fundamental work, the first part giving valuable commentary on bibliographies and other aids to historical research and the second surveying European historiography from the Renaissance to the end of the eighteenth century. Reprint of the second edition of 1901-04. (Mudge-Winchell, *Guide to Reference Books,* 7th ed. 1951) (D 4)

DICTIONNAIRE CRITIQUE, LITTERAIRE ET BIBLIOGRAPHIQUE DES PRIN-CIPAUX LIVRES CONDAMNÉS AU FEU, SUPRIMÉS OU CENSURÉS. G. Peignot. 2 Vols. 729 pp.* $24.00

The most complete collection and bibliography of original sources and invaluable information about books condemned to burning, suppression and censure for political, social and religious reasons. Reprint of 1806 edition. (D 2)

PROLEGOMENA TO THE HISTORY OF THE BYZANTINE EMPIRE. Constantine Amantos. Translated by Kenneth Johnstone with a Preface by Constantine Trypanis. 244 pp., approx. LC 67-17584. $10.00

With the ever rising interest of historians and the reading public in the long neglected history of the Byzantine Empire, the need for an introductory work explaining the reasons for the Hellenization of the Eastern Roman Empire and its subsequent rise to prominence in arts, letters and scholarship during the darkest historical period for the peoples of Western Europe is more than apparent. (D 2)

A HISTORY OF THE LATER ROMAN EMPIRE FROM ARCADIUS TO IRENE (395 A.D.-800 A.D.). J. B. Bury. 2 Vols. 1117 pp. $30.00

Reprint of the most complete and informative edition (1889) of a monumental reference work. NOT TO BE CONFUSED WITH OTHER EDITIONS COVERING ONLY THE PERIOD 395 to 565 A.D. (D—)

SELECTED ESSAYS. J. B. Bury; H. Temperly, editor. 250 pp. $10.50

Reprint of the *Corpus* edition (1930) of the essays and articles of the great historian which are so important for reference, such as *The Constitution of the Later Roman Empire*, 1909. Indispensable for students of the later Roman Empire and Early Byzantine history. (D—)

BYZANTINE TRADITION IN CHURCH EMBROIDERY. Pauline Johnstone. Quarto. 140 pp. + 121 plates. LC 67-17572 $14.00

A beautifully illustrated survey of Byzantine church embroideries and their influence on works of later periods by an expert on the subject who is also the author of a book on the needlework of the Greek islands. (D2)

INTRODUCTION TO EAST ROMAN COINAGE. J. F. Lhotka, Jr. 107 pp., illus. + 5 plates* $4.00

The best introductory work in English for those wishing to study the coinage of Byzantium and its western and barbaric imitations. Includes dynastic tables, analyses of types and inscriptions and bibliography. (A—)

IMPERIAL BYZANTINE COINS. A Catalogue of the Collection in the British Museum. Warwick Wroth. cxii + 688 + 79 plates. LC 66-19329. $50.00

A reprint of the most excellent and thorough reference work ever produced for the study and identification of the coinage of the Byzantine Empire. An introduction of about 100 pages provides a brief history of Byzantium with notes on the emperors, their families, and the dating and metals used in their coinage. The balance of the book is devoted to a chronological listing of the coins in the British Museum collection with their weight, metal, size, obverse and reverse inscriptions, types and date. There are four indices: emperors and dynasts, mints, general, inscriptions, and two appendices: alphabetical and chronological listings of the emperors, followed by tables converting inches to metric measure and English grams to French weights. The 79 plates picture nearly 1400 of the more representative coins. The original two volumes are bound as one for easier reference use. (D—)

WESTERN AND PROVINCIAL BYZANTINE COINS IN THE BRITISH MUSEUM. Vandals, Ostrogoths, Lombards, and the Empires of Thessalonica, Nicaea and Trebizond. Warwick Wroth. 438 + 48 plates. LC 66-25814. $25.00

The third volume in the corpus of Byzantine coins in the British Museum reissued, has all the western Imperial issues and the imitative coin types issued by the Vandals, Ostrogoths, etc., with excellent plates. An extremely valuable reference work, especially for the "splinter" empires which arose after the conquest of Constantinople by the Crusaders in 1204 and the division of the Byzantine Empire. The coins issued in local mints of the Emperors of Thessalonica, Nicaea, etc., are so similar to the Imperial issues that identification is nearly impossible without the illustrations in this volume. Contains a lengthy historical introduction, lists of emperors, mints, etc. and is indexed with extreme care. A "must" for the collector of the Byzantine series. (D—)

LETTRES DE L'EMPEREUR MANUEL II PALÉOLOGUE (1391-1423). Emile Legrand, editor. xii + 112 pp. $5.00

Reprint of the first edition (1893) of the letters of Manuel II Palaeologus, one of the most prominent emperors of the restored Byzantine empire. Letter texts are in Greek. (D—)

THE LASCARIDS OF NICAEA. The Story of an Empire in Exile. Alice Gardner. 321 pp. + 8 plates + 1 map $10.50

After the Frankish conquest of Constantinople, three Greek "empires" came into being, the most important of which was the Empire of Nicaea (1204-1261), which finally reconquered Constantinople and reestablished the Byzantine empire. This is the primary reference work on this period, and indispensable for any major library. Reprint of the 1912 edition. (D—)

GLOSSARIUM AD SCRIPTORES MEDIAE ET INFIMAE GRAECITATIS. Du Cange. Quarto. 2 Vols. bound in 1. 1280 pp. $50.00

The standard reference lexicon for Byzantine and Post-Byzantine Greek. Reprint of the 1688 edition. ". . . indispensable aid of the student of history and literature of the middle ages," *Encyclopaedia Britannica.* (A—)

A HANDBOOK OF GREEK AND LATIN PALAEOGRAPHY. Edward Maunde Thompson. 360 pp., illus. LC 66-19175. $10.00

A reprint of the classic book on this subject. Extensively illustrated with facsimilies of manuscripts of all periods with charts showing the development of writing techniques, information of the dating of manuscripts and an analysis of symbols and abbreviations. An indispensable reference. (D—)

NOTES ON ABBREVIATIONS IN GREEK MANUSCRIPTS. T. W. Allen. 40 pp. + 11 plates $3.50

Reprint of Oxford 1889 edition. (D 1)

MONNAIES BYZANTINES. Count I. Tolstoi. Quarto. 1060 pp. + 72 plates $70.00

Considered by all historians and numismatists to be the best work on Byzantine coins for the period 479 to 867 A.D. Reprint of the first edition (1912-1914) in Russian. (D 4)

INTRODUCTION À LA NUMISMATIQUE BYZANTINE. Henri Longuet. ix + 158 + 24 plates. $12.00

A concise introduction, in French, to Byzantine numismatics with historical commentary on coin-types, metals, legends, values, influence on other coinage, etc. and a chronological summary of the Byzantine Empire. (A—)

MONNAIES BYZANTINES. R. Ratto. 151 + 68 plates + pricelist. $15.00

Reprint of a famous auction catalogue of a unique collection of Byzantine Imperial coins and Western and Provincial issues. Many rare types are known only from the specimens listed and illustrated in this catalogue. (A—)

A HANDBOOK OF THE COINAGE OF THE BYZANTINE EMPIRE. Hugh Goodacre. 361 pp., illus. $16.00

A reprint in one volume of the 3 parts first published in 1928-33. A popularized account of Byzantine coinage and a catalogue of the most characteristic coin types prepared for those without a background in the classics who, nonetheless, wish to study Byzantine coins. (A—)

DESCRIPTION GÉNÉRALE DES MONNAIES BYZANTINES. J. Sabatier. 722 + 70 plates. $30.00

A reprint of the earliest (1862) reference book on Byzantine numismatics. Still useful and helpful for the serious researcher and historian and necessary for reference libraries. (C—)

BYZANTINE NUMISMATIC BIBLIOGRAPHY 1950—1965. JOEL L. MALTER. A systematic bibliography covering fifteen years of important publications on Byzantine numismatics and related subjects. Includes an introductory survey on the development of research in the major fields of Byzantine numismatics from 1950 —1965 *64 pages* $ 5.00

CONSTANTINE PALAEOLOGUS: THE LAST EMPEROR OF BYZANTIUM. CHEDOMIL MIJATOVICH. "We will not surrender the City to you." A tragic story of the last years of the Byzantine Empire and its last emperor who died fighting on the walls of Constantinople. Reprint of the 1892 edition. *xiv + 239 pp.* $ 10.00

CATALOGUE OF THE GREEK MANUSCRIPTS ON MOUNT ATHOS. Sp. P. Lambros. 2 Vols. Quarto. ix + 438 & vii + 597 $70.00

The unique list of the most important libraries of Byzantine and post-Byzantine manuscripts on Mount Athos, many of which never have been published. A work necessary to any study of ancient and Byzantine philology, literature and palaeography. Reprint of the edition 1895-1900. (D—)

ENGLISH SILVER COINAGE FROM 1649. H. A. Seaby and **P. A. Rayner.**
136 pp., illus. $3.50

The 2nd edition of the standard reference work. Each coin type is described and every date and main variety is listed and tabulated for easy reference. (C—)

THE COINAGE OF SCOTLAND. A HANDBOOK. J. D. Robertson. xxx +
146 pp. $7.00

An excellent numismatic work describing every variety of gold, silver, billon and copper coin issued by the Scottish mint from Alexander I (1107-1124) to Anne Stuart (1714). Reprint of the rare 1878 edition. (D 4)

Subscription price until June 30, 1967—$5.00.

LES MÉDAILLEURS ITALIENS DES QUINZIEME ET SEIZIEME SIÈCLES. A.
Armand 3 Vols.* 1073 pp., illus. $48.00

This classic work is considered the *corpus* of Italian Renaissance medals. The detailed descriptions, accurate measurements and the stylistic analyses of scenes, persons and inscriptions are of importance to art historians and numismatists and will make it possible to identify later imitations and falsifications. (D—)

THE COINAGE OF IRELAND from the Invasion of the Danes to the Reign of
George IV. John Lindsay. Quarto. iv + 144 pp. + 22 plates $20.00

Reprint in a limited edition of this very rare reference work (1839) which remains to date the most complete book on Irish coinage. No more than 10 copies of the small original edition are known to exist in American libraries. (D 3)

CASTLES ON THE RHINE. M.J. MEHS. A view of
the Rhineland during medieval times with emphasis on the
history and architecture of the castles along the Rhine and
their owners. Amply illustrated with excellent photographs
and contemporary engravings of the castles and the sur-
rounding countryside. *72 pages, illustrated, 39 plates   paper covers* $ 2.50

HANDBUCH DER POLNISCHEN NUMISMATIK. Marian Gumowski. 240 pp.
+ 56 plates + 1 map $15.00

This handbook of Polish numismatics is the unique handy reference for the collector of Polish coins. 1960 German translation of the Polish original published in 1914. (D—)

CATALOGUE DE LA COLLECTION DES MÉDAILLES ET MONNAIES POLO-
NAISES. Emeryk Hutten-Czapski. Quarto. 5 Vols. bound in 3. 2272 pp.
+ 29 plates $75.00

The primary reference work on Polish coins and medals with long commentaries on the history, genaeology and heraldry of Poland. Reprint of the 1871-1916 edition. (D—)

LE MONETE E LE BOLLE PLUMBEE PONTIFICIE DEL MEDAGLIERE VATI-
CANO. Count Camillo Serafini. 4 Vols. 1797 pp. + 227 plates* $192.00

Reprint of the best reference work to date (1910-1928) describing and classifying papal medals, coins and lead seals from the earliest specimens through 1928. (D—)

A DESCRIPTIVE CATALOGUE OF PAPAL MEDALS. 123 pp., illus. $4.00

A reissue of the 1898 edition cataloguing all known ancient, medieval and modern medals from St. Peter (45 A.D.) through Leo XIII (1878-1903). Over 2300 medals listed. (A—)

A START TO COIN COLLECTING. ENGLISH COINS ELIZABETH II to
CHARLES II (1660). Margaret Amstell. 78 pp., illus. $3.50

An introduction to the collecting of English coins with emphasis on inexpensive issues for the beginner. Easy to read, but containing information also of value to an expert. (B—)

ENGLISH HAMMERED COINAGE. J. J. North.
Vol. I. 202, illus. + 16 plates. $14.00   Vol. II. 195 + 10 plates. $12.00

Volume I contains a catalogue of mints and moneyers of early Britain listing all minting towns with charts of early alphabet variations, crosses, monograms, etc. Bibliography. Vol. II lists an additional 2700 coins with ecclesiastical mints, translations of legends, etc. This set covers the period from early Anglo-Saxon coinage. (c. 650) through that of Charles II (1662). (A—)

THE COINS OF THE HAPSBURG EMPERORS and Related Issues 1619 - 1919.
R. Selwyn Mort. 179 + plates, map. $10.00

For the first time the student of the history of the Austro-Hungarian Empire during the rule of the Hapsburgs can have readily available the numismatic issues and evidence related to the historical events of each ruler. Also, the collector of the coins of the Hapsburgs will find this an excellent guide for organizing and studying his collection. (C—)

TRAITÉ DE NUMISMATIQUE MODERNE ET CONTEMPORAINE. A. Engel & R. Serrure. 2 vols. in 1*. 800 pp., illus. $45.00

Reprint of the basic reference work (1897-1899) completing and continuing the treatise on medieval numismatics by the same authors. This is the cornerstone of modern numismatic studies and is unsurpassed by any more recent work. (D—)

NUMISMATISCHES WAPPEN-LEXICON. W. Rentzmann. viii + 113 + 283 plates. $25.00

Reprint of the renowned and much in demand reference work (1876) for collectors of modern coins, especially crowns and thalers, who wish to identify and interpret the heraldic symbols on family, city and state crests. A unique tool for the student of heraldry as it pictures well over 5000 different crests. (B—)

NUMISMATISCHES LEGENDEN-LEXICON. W. Rentzmann. viii + 191 + 247 + 46. $20.00

A companion to the *Wappen-Lexicon* these 3 volumes reprinted in one interpret all known coin inscriptions of medieval and modern Europe with dynastic tables and dates and other unique information on money-issuing rulers. A complete list of names of cities, states and mints appearing on coins makes this book an indispensable tool for any student of modern coins. Absolutely necessary for major public and university libraries. (B—)

THE SILVER BENELUX. A.DELMONTE. A catalogue of all larger silver coins struck in the Benelux territories, down to the ¼ daalder. This is an entirely new catalogue and is the most complete to be published to date. *318 pages, 52 plates*   *8½ x 11*   *$ 25.00*

COINS AND MEDALS OF THE STATE OF THE IONIAN ISLANDS including the Venetian Issues and the Provisional Issues under English Occupation. Paul Lambros. viii + 48 + 6 plates $4.00

Translated from the Greek original (1884) and enlarged with a special chapter on Venetian issues. A unique treatise important for the study of the period 1700-1811. (D 2)

THE COINAGE OF MODERN GREECE, CRETE, THE IONIAN ISLANDS AND CYPRUS (1700 - 1967). S. Gardiakos. viii + 96 pp., illus. + 16 plates. $7.50

The first book covering this subject and the first complete list of issues and varieties available to date. Maps, tables and illustrations of the coins, plus a special insert of current market values makes this book a must for the numismatist and modern historian. (D 3)

ALBANIAN HISTORICAL FOLKSONGS 1716– 1943. PYRRHUS J. RUCHES. The unique collection of Albanian folk poetry published to date, with the original Albanian songs and facing English translations. The text describes the origins, historical significance and imagery of the songs. *ix + 126 pages*   *$ 7.50*

SCANDENBERG (GEORGES CASTRIOTA). ESSAI DE BIBLIOGRAPHIE RAISONNÉE. G. T. Petrovitch. xixx + 188 pp. $15.00

A complete listing of works, articles and essays in all languages on Scanderberg, the brightest historical figure of the fight against the Turks in the highlands of Albania and Epirus (1443-67). Reprint of Paris 1881 edition. (D 2)

THE GREEK WAR OF INDEPENDENCE 1821 - 1833. General Theodore Kolokotronis. Translated by **E. M. Edmonds.** 360 pp. LC 65-26126. $10.00

A reprint of the famous English translation (*Kolokotronis: Klepht & Warrior*) of the memoirs of one of the greatest leaders of the Greek Revolution against Turkish oppression and occupation. A stirring record of heroism and the desperate fight for freedom by a handful of warriors against the hordes of the Ottoman Empire. The story is as related to George Tertzetis, first librarian of the Greek Parliament, by the author, after the liberation of Greece. (D 3)

AMERICANS IN THE GREEK REVOLUTION. GEORGE JARVIS: HIS JOURNAL AND RELATED DOCUMENTS. G. G. Arnakis and **E. Demetracopoulou.** xxxii + 282. illus.* LC 66-20437. $8.00

A first hand report of the Greek War of Independence as recorded by George Jarvis in his journal and letters. Jarvis was a New Yorker who enlisted in the Greek army in which he attained the rank of lieutenant general. This is one of the most important American documents related to the War of Independence in Greece. (D—)

JACKRABBITS TO JETS. The History of North Island, San Diego, California. ELRETTA SUDSBURY.

This book traces the history of flight as it developed at North Island beginning with the Curtis era (1911) and it sketches the evolution of aircraft from the A-1 Triad to the latest jets. An important reference work for all interested in the history of aviation. Numerous photographs showing major aircraft types from 1911 to 1967. *x + 411 pages, illustrated*   *8½ x 11*   *$ 20.00*

EARLY HALF DOLLAR DIE VARIETIES. AL C.. OVERTON.

An important reference work for the student of the United States coinage of 1794-1836. Contains a descriptive analysis and catalogue of all half dollars with lettered edges and liberty busts, and their many varieties. *xvi + 349 pages, illustrated*   *$ 12.50*

AMERICANS IN THE GREEK REVOLUTION. GEORGE JARVIS: HIS JOURNAL AND RELATED DOCUMENTS. G. G. Arnakis and E. Demetracopoulou. xxxii + 282. illus.* LC 66-20437. $8.00

A first hand report of the Greek War of Independence as recorded by George Jarvis in his journal and letters. Jarvis was a New Yorker who enlisted in the Greek army in which he attained the rank of lieutenant general. This is one of the most important American documents related to the War of Independence in Greece. (D—)

BRITISH AND AMERICAN PHILHELLENES IN THE GREEK WAR OF INDEPENDENCE 1821 - 1833. Douglas Dakin. 248 + plates.* LC 56-58873. $7.00

A complete reference book examining all the known British and American philhellenes who helped fight for the freedom of Greece. The author has used original sources (many in modern Greek) to present a vivid chronicle of the contributions to Greek independence by these volunteers. With a complete list of known participants plus a section of plates with portraits, sketches and maps. (D—)

BIBLIOTHECA AMERICANA VETUSTISSIMA. A Description of Works Relating to America Published Between the Years 1492 and 1551. H. HARRISSE.

A study of the earliest books and manuscripts about America with extensive commentaries on their authors and editors. There are references to the many editions of there works, descriptions of their actual appearance, and in most cases, facsimile reproductions of entire pages or portions thereof. No other bibliography covering this period and subject has delved so deeply into the background of the works, their various editions and their authors. Reprint of the 1866/1872 edition. *2 volumes in 1. liv + 519 pages & xl + 199 pages, facsimile illustrations*   *$ 50.00*

THE EARLY COINS OF AMERICA AND THE LAWS GOVERNING THEIR ISSUE. SYLVESTER

S. CROSBY. *ix + 378 pages + 10 plates*   *$ 25.00*

CIVIL WAR TOKENS AND TRADESMEN'S STORE CARDS. GEORGE HETRICH AND JULIUS

GUTTAG with a supplement by JOSEPH BARNET. *321 pages + 16 plates*   *7 x 10*   *$ 15.00*

ANTIQUITATES AMERICANAE. Societas regia antiquariorum SF., editors.
Folio xl + 479 pp. + 18 plates, 8 in color. $37.50

A collection of texts prior to 1492 referring to America given in the original Norwegian and Danish with Latin translations and including the chronicles of Greenland and Vinland. Manuscript facsimiles and runic inscriptions illustrated in the plates. Basic necessity for all Americana collections, especially those of universities. Particularly interesting for students of the Yale map published in 1965. Reprint of 1837 edition. (D 1)

BIBLIOTHECA AMERICANA VETUSTISSIMA. H. Harisse. 2 Vols. in 1 liv + 519 pp. & xl + 199 pp. $50.00

A most rare bibliography and description of books of the "early Americana" group. Describes all known works relative to America published between the years 1492 and 1551. Anastatic reprint of the edition 1866-72. (A 2)

THE AMERICAN INDIAN FRONTIER

WILLIAM CHRISTIE MACLEOD

" . . . this volume represents the first attempt at an analysis of American frontier history made particularly from the viewpoint of the Indian side of our frontier development." (from the Preface). Necessary to every collection of Americana. Reprint of the 1928 edition.

xxiii + 598 pp. *$ 30.00*

THE CIVILIZATION OF THE SOUTH AMERICAN INDIANS (with special reference to Magic and Religion)

RAFAEL KARSTEN with a Preface by EDWARD WESTERMARCK

An anthropological and sociological study of the South American Indians with special emphasis on their religion and their superstitious beliefs and practices. The author lived among the Indians of Argentina, Bolivia and Ecuador for seven years and derived his theories from personal inquiry as well as a study of earlier writings in an effort to understand the primitive customs and beliefs of the Indians. Reprint of the 1926 edition.

xxxii + 540 pp. *$ 30.00*

BIBLIOTHÈQUE AMERICAINE. H. Ternaux-Compans. viii + 191 pp. $15.00

Reprint of the 1837 catalogue of books and studies related to America published from 1492 to 1700. (D 1)

JEAN ET SEBASTIEN CABOT. H. Harisse. 400 pp., illus. $30.00

Reprint of a standard French work (1882) examining the voyages of John and Sebastian Cabot. An historical and critical study accompanied by maps, bibliography and chronology of their travels to the Northwest from 1497 to 1550. (D 2)

THE ENTERPRISING COLONIALS. SOCIETY ON THE EVE OF REVOLUTION. William S. Sachs and Ari Hoogenboom. 256 pp., illus., tables, maps. LC 65-15466. $8.50

"In a crisp style . . . the authors of this widely researched book survey colonial history in terms of the rise of American business . . . The author's findings have far-reaching implications for the interpretation of the American Revolution . . . a provocative and important book." *New York State Historical Society.* (D—)

JOHN HENRY. A FOLK-LORE STUDY. L. W. Chappell. 144 pp. $5.00

Reprint of the 1933 edition of a unique study of the John Henry tradition in the South. A combination of Paul Bunyan and Robin Hood, John Henry is one of America's most interesting folk-heroes, known variously as a steel-driver, tunnel worker, etc., who became a legend after the Civil War. An appendix contains the most important versions of the folk-songs and ballads known to date. (D—)

FORTHCOMING BOOKS

BYZANTINE STUDIES. Robert Lopez. *300 pages, approx. (D)* $ 10.00

For the first time, collected in one volume, nine outstanding papers by the Chairman of Mediaeval Studies at Yale University, on the economic history of Byzantium from the fourth to the fourteenth century. Essential reading for all students of the period. Among the papers included are: *Byzantine Law in the Seventh Century and its Reception by the Germans and the Arabs, The Silk Industry in the Byzantine Empire, The Dollar of the Middle Ages, The Role of Trade in the Economic Readjustment of Byzantium in the Seventh Century, Harmenopoulos and the Downfall of the Bezant.*

TREBIZOND. THE LAST GREEK EMPIRE. William Miller. *viii + 140 pages. (D)* $ 6.00

The finest work to date on the Empire of the Trebizond, the independent Greek state founded in 1204 with the dynasty of the "Great Comneni." Contains a new preface and bibliography by Anastasius Bandy, Professor of Classics at the University of California at Riverside. RR1926.

A HISTORY OF THE ICONOCLASTIC CONTROVERSY. E. J. Martin. *282 pages (D)*
    $ 10.00

The standard work on the religious controversy which characterized the epoch (711-843) and caused internal strife in the Byzantine Empire for over a century. With an introduction by Professor John Anastos. RR1930.

LEGENDS OF THE RHINELAND. August Antz. 100 pages, illustrated. (D) $ 2.25

Fifty seven legends and folktales from the Rhine region, translated by Kathlyn Rutherford. Especially interesting to students of medieval folklore and the survival of ancient customs in modern times.

THE COINAGE OF THE TULUNI DYNASTY. Edward T. Rogers. *8½ x 11. 22 pages + 1 plate (D*)* $ 2.00

A catalogue of Moslem coins of the Tulun dynasty founded in the ninth century.

A MANUAL OF MUSALMAN NUMISMATICS. O. Codrington. *viii + 239 pages + 2 plates. (D)* $ 10.00

A handbook of Musalman coins especially intended for those who do not know Arabic or Persian. Contains extensive sections on these alphabets, the legends and titles which appear on these coins (with English translations), lists of mint towns in Arabic with English equivalents and geographic locations, etc. An essential reference book for anyone dealing with this branch of Oriental numismatics. R1904.

THE COINAGE OF THE EUROPEAN CONTINENT. W. CAREW HAZLITT. *554 pages, illustrated.*   *In Preparation* $ 30.00

This book contains a most useful survey of European coinage and three catalogues: Hundreds of European Mints, An exhaustive list of European denominations and European rulers including names , year of accession, etc. of over 2000 kings, princes, dukes, counts, and other rulers. A reprint including the supplement issued in 1897.

SIEGE AND NECESSITY COINS OF THE WORLD. PROSPER MAILLIET. *2 Volumes*
Atlas of Coins: 206 plates   8½ x 11
Text to the Atlas: 832 pages   5½ x 8½
In Preparation — The Set $ 50.00

The standard reference work on siege and necessity coins with over 2,000 coins illustrated. This is a reprint of *Catalogue descriptif des monnaies obsidionales et de necessite* which, although in French, is so arranged as to make it easy to follow for English readers as well.

THE OTTOMAN EMPIRE AND ITS TRIBUTARY STATES (excepting Egypt) with a Sketch of Greece. W. S. Cooke. *viii + 195 pages + 3 foldout maps in colour (D)*   15.00

A survey of the Ottoman Empire with special sections on Tunis and Tripoli, Bulgaria and Bosnia-Herzogovina, Romania, Serbia, Montenegro and Greece. Special emphasis on the military strength and organization of the Turks in the nineteenth century. R1876.

HISTORY OF THE ISLAND OF CORFU and of the Republic of the Ionian Islands. Henry Jervis-White Jervis. *xii + 323 pages, illus. + foldout plate.* $ 11.00

A history of Corfu from ancient times through the nineteenth century and of the Ionian Islands during the period of British authority. R1852.

GREEK HISTORICAL FOLKSONGS. Klephtic Ballads. John W. Baggally. *xiv + 110 pages. (D)* $ 7.50

The stories of the various Greek rebellions prior to the War of Independence of 1821 and legends of their leaders have been preserved in the oral tradition by the people of the Greek mountains and islands. Baggally was the first to collect the most important of these historical folksongs and to translate them. This book presents these songs with an important historical commentary on each one. A classic study in the pre-revolutionary history of modern Greece. R1936.

THE ARGONAUT LIBRARY OF ANTIQUITIES

Standard Reference Works on Greek Art and Numismatics

MASTERPIECES OF GREEK SCULPTURE. Adolf Furtwängler. xvi + 439, illus. + 24 plates. LC 64-910. $20.00

A reissue of the first systematic work (1895) on the works and styles of the great Greek masters, considered to be the fundamental reference for any modern study. The originals and ancient copies in the great museums and art galleries of the world identified as the works of Pheidias, Praxiteles, Polykleitos, Skopas, etc. are carefully analyzed stylistically and the most famous appear in the 300 text illustrations and the 24 plates of the new edition. New select bibliography, notes and indices. (D—)

ANCIENT COINS ILLUSTRATING LOST MASTERPIECES OF GREEK ART— NUMISMATIC COMMENTARY ON PAUSANIAS. F. Imhoof-Blumer and Percy Gardner. lxxx + 176 + 32 plates. LC 64-23435. $10.00

A new enlarged edition of a long out of print work (1885-7) important for the study of numismatic sources related to the history of Greek sculpture and Greek art in general. On the basis of the detailed descriptions of famous works of art by Pausanias, the authors identified the representations of the works on Greek coins. In this way a unique gallery of destroyed, lost or yet undiscovered great works of art has been formed, showing us what once adorned the cities and shrines of ancient Greece. (D—)

THE ELDER PLINY'S CHAPTERS ON THE HISTORY OF ART. K. Jex-Blake and Eugenie Sellers Strong. c + 252. LC 66-19183. $10.00

A reissue of another basic reference work for the history of Greek sculpture much in demand since 1896. Updated with a new introduction and select bibliography by R. V. Schoder, S.J. of Loyola University. Pliny's original texts are accompanied by long commentaries on what ancient sculptures have been identified on the basis of his writings. (D 2)

ANCIENT WRITERS ON GREEK SCULPTURE. H. Stuart Jones. 320 pp. LC 65-26123. $10.00

A reprint of this long out of print reference work (1895) enlarged with a new preface, bibliographically updated and carefully indexed for the first time. Includes all the basic passages and references from the classical authors which are necessary for the study of Greek sculpture. The original texts are given with English translations and commentaries. (D—)

ANCIENT GREEK AND ROMAN BRONZES. Winifred Lamb. 360 pp., illus., plates. LC 67-17575. $10.00

The most widely acclaimed reference work on ancient bronze works of art, long out of print and unavailable. Illustrated with a fine selection of bronzes from museums and galleries around the world and accompanied by an instructive and well documented text, this work is rightfully considered the basic source in all courses and seminars on ancient art. Enlarged with an introduction and select bibliography by Dr. Lenore Keene Congdon. (D 3)

ALEXANDER THE GREAT IN GREEK AND ROMAN ART. Margaret Bieber. 108 + 64 plates. LC 64-23430. $7.50

A new work of important reference value examining all the known portraits of the great conqueror made during his lifetime and later during the Hellenistic and Roman periods. The plates illustrate 122 examples of sculpture, bronzes, gems and coins. The lengthy fully documented text, together with many plates, make this monograph the best introduction to Hellenistic and Roman art written by one of the foremost authorities in the field. (D—)

ANCIENT GREEK DRESS. Ethel Abrahams and Lady Evans. xx + 228, illus. + 48 plates. LC 64-23436. $7.50

A new volume combining for the first time the two basic reference works for the study of ancient Greek dress in the English language with a new introduction, select bibliography, notes and many new illustrations of works of Greek art from all over the world. Considered to be an indispensable reference work by the reviewers of *Library Journal, The Classical Journal* and many leading classical scholars. (D—)

SELECT NUMISMATIC BIBLIOGRAPHY. Elvira Clain-Stefanelli. xiv + 406 pp.   **$12.50**

The first extensive bibliography of its kind, compiled by the AssociateCurator of Numismatics in the Smithsonian Institution. Critical listings of all the most important works on numismatics in all languages,covering ancient, mediaeval and modern coinage, paper money, medals and early and primitive forms of money. Indispensable for reference rooms in all public and university libraries. (D—)

A BIBLIOGRAPHY OF APPLIED NUMISMATICS IN THE FIELDS OF GREEK AND ROMAN ARCHAEOLOGY AND THE FINE ARTS. Cornelius C. Vermeule. viii + 172. $4.00

A most useful list of over 1300 works demonstrative of the usefulness of numismatic evidence in classical archaeology and the fine arts. The material is especially helpful to anyone wishing to locate references in fields in which numismatics are fundamental for the understanding of non-numismatic problems. (A—)

THE PADUANS: MEDALS BY GIOVANNI CAVINO. Richard Hoe Lawrence. 31 pp., illus.* $1.50

A book enabling the neophyte or advanced collector to identify the well-executed imitations of Roman medals made by the skilled Renaissance artist Giovanni Cavino. (C—)

BECKER THE COUNTERFEITER. George F. Hill. 111 + 19 plates. $12.00

A reprint of the brief biography of this nineteenth century counterfeiter of ancient coins, followed by a detailed list of illustrations of 361 of Becker's counterfeits for immediate identification. Becker was one of the most expert counterfeiters of ancient coins ever known and even some of the experts have been deceived by his work. (A—)

A GEOGRAPHIC LEXICON OF GREEK COIN INSCRIPTIONS. A. Florance. 112 pp. LC 66-19173. $5.00

The first American publication of this handy lexicon identifying both the abbreviated and complete ethnics (inscriptions) of the Greek city-states inscribed on their coins, most of which are not found in the usual Greek lexicons. Each has an indication of the general area in which the city was located, and in the case of the Greek Imperial issues, the province of the Roman Empire. With maps of ancient Greece and Rome plus lists of cities which issued non-inscribed coins and coins with bilingual inscriptions. A basic tool for any student of Greek archaeology and philology and the numismatist. (D—)

A DICTIONARY OF GREEK COIN INSCRIPTIONS. Severin Icard. Limited edition of 450 numbered copies. xlviii + 564 + 2 plates. $30.00

A limited edition of the famous lexicographical work *Identification des Monnaies par la Nouvelle méthode des lettres-jalons et des Légendes Fragmentées* in which are included all known Greek coin inscriptions. The introduction appears in an English translation. In the corpus all inscriptions, complete and fragmentary, of kings, emperors, mint officials, generals, states, cities, etc. are listed alphabetically with descriptive epithets in many cases. A major reference work and an invaluable help in identifying coins. Each word of the inscription is also listed separately for easy identification in the case of worn or partially destroyed inscriptions. (D 2)

ANCIENT, MEDIEVAL, MODERN COINS AND HOW TO KNOW THEM. Gertrude B. Rawlings. xix + 360 + 30 plates. LC 66-19186. $10.00

A reprint of a much in demand manual which is an introduction to the history and development of coins and coinage from the earliest period to the first decade of the 20th century. A valuable book for those specializing in one period of coinage who wish to extend their knowledge to another. (D—)

COINS AND MEDALS: THEIR PLACE IN HISTORY AND ART. Stanley Lane Poole. 200 pp., approx., illus. LC 66-19182. $10.00

A reissue, with new typesetting, of the 1885 edition containing essays on the ancient coins of Europe and Asia by the editors of the famed British Museum catalogues of coins. Excellent introduction in one handy volume to the following coins: ancient Greek, Roman, Indian, Japanese, Chinese, Mohammedan, Phoenician, Parthian, Judaean, Sassanian, Nabathean, early English and the coinage of Christian Europe, plus a chapter on medals. (D 2)

COIN TYPES. THEIR ORIGIN AND DEVELOPMENT 700 B.C. — 1604 A.D. Sir George Macdonald. 286 pp., illus. + 16 plates. LC 67-17581. $10.00

A reprint of the famous and much in demand text of the author's lectures on the history of coins (1905). A book designed for the average reader, but due to the importance, validity and originality of its contents, it has been raised to a prominent position among numismatic reference books. Important for the study of the history, problems and general background of numismatics beginning with the most primitive coinage of the ancient world through Byzantium, the medieval period, the Renaissance and the dawn of modern world coinage. (D 2)

HISTORIA NUMORUM: A MANUAL OF GREEK NUMISMATICS. Barclay V. Head. lxxxviii + 978, illus. $30.00

Reprinted from the 1911 edition, this manual remains a masterpiece of numismatic scholarship. The author produced a handbook in one volume containing in condensed form a complete and detailed sketch of the numismatic history of nearly every city, king or dynast known to have struck coins in the ancient Greek world. Considered by Shaw (List of Books for College Libraries, p. 32) to be the basic reference volume on Greek numismatics. With 7 indices and an extensive reference bibliography. (D 2)

THE ILLUSTRATIONS OF THE HISTORIA NUMORUM. Barclay V. Head and N. Svoronos. Royal octavo. 64 pp. + 40 plates $7.50

Users of the famous Historia Numorum in all its English editions have long agreed that if it lacks anything it is illustrations of the most famous coins described in it. Very few know that Barclay Head actually prepared a set of 35 plates illustrating about 420 coins in obverse and reverse which, with their descriptions, formed the third volume of the modern Greek translation of Historia Numorum published in Athens in 1898 by the also famous numismatist Nicholas Svoronos.

This small volume is now reprinted with the addition of 5 plates and is a necessary addition to each copy of Historia Numorum already in any library or personal collection. (D 4)

ANCIENT GREEK AND ROMAN COINS: A HANDBOOK. George F. Hill. xvi + 296, illus. + 16 plates. LC 64-23439. $10.00

The fundamental introductory work (1899) to the coinages of the ancient world, now reissued with a new bibliography and other addenda. Ideal for the student of archaeology and the collector of ancient coins. The most important coins are catalogued and illustrated. (D—)

ANCIENT ARCHITECTURE ON GREEK AND ROMAN COINS AND MEDALS; ARCHITECTURA NUMISMATICA. T. L. Donaldson. 382 + 54 plates. LC 65-15464. $10.00

A reprint of a very valuable and unique collection (1856) of the representations of ancient temples, shrines, theatres, public buildings, city walls, gates, bridges, etc. illustrated on ancient coins and medals issued in Greece and Rome. These architectural monuments are seen on the coins in the state of preservation in which they existed when the coins were struck, thus giving us an excellent record of ancient architecture, much of which is now lost, destroyed or unexcavated. With a new select annotated bibliography, introduction, biographical note of the author and a detailed index. (D—)

HISTORICAL GREEK COINS. George F. Hill. xxvi + 182 + 16 plates. LC 66-19179. $10.00

An excellent and methodical numismatic commentary to the highlights of the history of ancient Greece from the rise of archaic Greece to the Persian Wars, from the brilliance of the Athenian Empire until its downfall in the Peloponnesian War and the decline of the city-states. Coins illuminate history most vividly here and illustrate the growth of Alexander's empire and the history of the Hellenistic states and kingdoms until the final conquest by Rome. (D—)

HISTORICAL ROMAN COINS. George F. Hill. xvi + 196 + 16 plates. LC 66-19180. $10.00

The companion volume to Historical Greek Coins, in which coins tell the story of Rome from the earliest period to the highlights of the Republic and its final submission to the Empire established during the rule of Augustus Octavianus. (D—)

THE COINS OF THE GREEK AND SCYTHIC KINGS OF BACTRIA AND INDIA. Percy Gardner. 272 pp. + 32 plates. LC 66-25813. $15.00

Originally issued in 1886 in an edition of just 300 copies, this amazing corpus of the historical coins minted by the Greek and Scythic kings of Bactria and India, appears again for the first time. This is the basic sourcebook for the chronicles of almost 200 years of the eastern-most Hellenistic empire, unknown from any other source. Planned and issued as the first volume of the Catalogue of Indian Coins in the British Museum, this rare reference work was expanded by the author to include coins from other museums and private collections. This edition has been enlarged by a preface, a select bibliography, and a new dynastic chart of the Greco-Bactrian kings according to the most recent authorities. (D—)

GREEK IMPERIAL COINS AND THEIR MINTS. Tom B. Jones. 112 pp., illus. LC 66-19174. $5.00

A new book tracing through coins for the first time the eastward expansion of the Roman Empire. A unique reference for the study of Greek inscribed Imperial coins issued in the Greek-speaking provinces. Also for the first time a complete list and map appear showing all the city mints known to date. Very little has been written on this coinage, making this book of especial importance to the historian and numismatist. (D 2)

GENERAL INFORMATION

All books in this catalogue are cloth bound except those marked by an asterisk (*). All books are 5½ x 8¼ or 6 x 9 unless otherwise noted. All books published and/or distributed by Argonaut Inc., Publishers may be ordered directly from the publisher or from any established book jobber, coin dealer or book store. Libraries and interested scholars are invited to participate in our STANDING ORDER PLAN. Details are available upon request and considerable savings may be realized.

ALL PRICES herein are retail and subject to change without notice. All prices are subject to trade discounts in accordance with our discount schedule available to bona fide dealers upon request. We are participants in the SCOP agreement of the ABA. ALL ORDERS for books already published and in stock are shipped the same day they are received. Orders for future books will be held pending publication. The publishers advise that advance payments will be held until publication of books or until out of stock books are available again. Full credits will be issued however toward the purchase of other books.

BOOKS AVAILABLE ARE SHIPPED IN 24 HOURS

ARGONAUT INC., PUBLISHERS

737 North Michigan Avenue

Chicago, Illinois 60611